The Floating Market

Ruth Price

This book belongs to

....

HODDER
EDUCATION
AN HACHETTE UK COMPANY

Lan was at the market.
She was helping Mum and Gran.

Talk about the story.
Who was at the market? Why did Lan have a box? Say where the bananas are. Say where the melons are. Why do you think Lan was smiling?

It was fun at the market.
Lan ran along by the boats.

Talk about the words.

What sort of market was it? What is the opposite of 'float'?
What else floats? How many signs can you see? Read them aloud.

Mum picked six big radishes and ten red chilli peppers. She paid the seller.

Talk about the story.

What did Mum buy? What else was the seller selling?
What would you buy?

Gran tipped the things into Lan's box.

Talk about the words.

Point to the chilli peppers in the picture. Are chilli peppers always red?
Say the letter name and sound for the fruits and vegetables in the picture.

Gran picked a big melon.
Mum paid the man.

Talk about the story.

What did Gran buy from the man? What was Mum doing?
How do you think Lan was feeling? Why?

Gran put the melon in Lan's box.

Talk about the words.

The melon was round and heavy. What other food is round and heavy?
What does Lan mean 'not much room'? What is another word for 'room'?

Mum picked a big bunch
of bananas. Gran paid.

Talk about the story.

*What did Mum buy? What was happening to Lan and the box?
Who noticed that Lan's box was getting heavy?*

Mum packed the bananas on top of Lan's box.

Talk about the words.

Mum bought a bunch of bananas. Clap the rhythm of 'bunch of bananas'. Say some other phrases that have the same rhythm.

Mum and Gran kept shopping.
Gran got the buns.

Can you pick me a bag of ten buns?

Talk about the story.

What did Gran buy? What was Mum buying?
Who was going to carry the buns and the flower?

Mum got a big, pink flower.

Talk about the words.

Gran got a bag of ten rice buns and Mum got a flower.
What is another word for 'got'? Describe the flower Mum bought.

Mum and Gran looked at the box and then at Lan.

The box is too full!

We got too much from the market!

Talk about the story.

Why can't Gran see Lan's face? Why were things falling out of the box? Why was it funny? Did Lan think it was funny?

They took the box from Lan and she had a bun.

Talk about the words.

Why did Mum say, 'Oh no'? What does 'too full' mean?
The box is too full. Say another word that has a long 'oo' in it, like 't-oo'.

Poems and rhymes

Chop, Chop

Chop, chop, choppity-chop,
Cut off the bottom,
And cut off the top.
What there is left we will
Put in the pot;
Chop, chop, choppity-chop.

By Anonymous

Make a Food Train

Water, water, water,
Rice and chicken, rice and chicken,
Rice and chicken, rice and chicken,
Ice cream and fruit, ice cream and fruit,
Ice cream and fruit, ice cream and fruit,
Bread and cheese, bread and cheese, bread and cheese,
Bread and cheese, bread and cheese, bread and cheese, full!

Adapted from Food Train by Julia Donaldson

Chant the poems.
Clap 'Chop, chop' as you chant it. In 'Make a Food Train', make the rhythm of the words sound like a train as you move along!

Mangoes and Pawpaws

Mangoes ripe and juicy,
Hanging from the tree,
Mangoes ripe and ready,
Go pick one for me.

Pawpaws ripe and juicy,
Hanging from the tree,
Pawpaws ripe and ready,
Go pick one for me.

*Adapted from a traditional
Caribbean rhyme*

Fruit for Tea

Coconuts, coconuts,
1, 2, 3,
We want coconuts –
Help us shake the tree!

Bananas, bananas,
1, 2, 3,
We want bananas –
Shake, shake, shake that tree!

Tangerines, tangerines,
1, 2, 3,
We want tangerines –
FOR OUR TEA!

By Ruth Price

Sing or say the poems.
Add two more verses to 'Mangoes and Pawpaws' with different fruits.
Shout the words in capitals in the last line of 'Fruit for Tea'.

Number the things to show the order Mum and Gran bought them. Then retell the story.

 Write a shopping list for Lan.

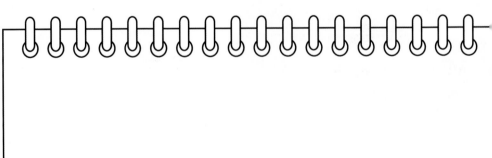